OCT 1 4

MACHINES AND WEAPONRY OF THE VIETNAM WAR

Charlie Samuels

Gareth Stevens
Publishing

Please visit our website, www.garethstevens.com. For a free color catalog of all our high-quality books, call toll free 1-800-542-2595 or fax 1-877-542-2596.

Library of Congress Cataloging-in-Publication Data

Samuels, Charlie, 1961-
 Machines and weaponry of the Vietnam war / Charlie Samuels.
    p. cm. — (Machines that won the war)
 Includes index.
 ISBN 978-1-4339-8600-0 (pbk.)
 ISBN 978-1-4339-8601-7 (6-pack)
 ISBN 978-1-4339-8599-7 (library binding)
 1. Vietnam War, 1961-1975—Equipment and supplies—Juvenile literature. 2. Military weapons—History—20th century—Juvenile literature. I. Title.
 DS559.8.S9S26 2013
 959.704'34—dc23
                        2012034541

Published in 2013 by
Gareth Stevens Publishing
111 East 14th Street, Suite 349
New York, NY 10003

© 2013 Brown Bear Books Ltd.

For Brown Bear Books Ltd:
Editorial Director: Lindsey Lowe
Managing Editor: Tim Cooke
Children's Publisher: Anne O'Daly
Art Director: Jeni Child
Designer: Lynne Lennon
Picture Manager: Sophie Mortimer
Picture Researcher: Andrew Webb

Picture Credits
Front Cover: U.S. Department of Defense

All photographs Library of Congress except: **Fly-By-Owen**: 11b; **Robert Hunt Library**: 6, 10, 15br, 38; **Shutterstock**: Darren Brode 22, RCP Photo 15t; **U.S. Department of Defense**: 8, 9tr, 32, 33, 36, 40, 41, 44.

Key: t = top, c = center, b = bottom, l = left, r = right.

Manufactured in the United States of America
1 2 3 4 5 6 7 8 9 12 11 10

CPSIA compliance information: Batch #CW13GS: For further information contact Gareth Stevens, New York, New York at 1-800-542-2595.

CONTENTS

INTRODUCTION

The Vietnam War was a continuation of a conflict that began in the 1950s between Vietnamese nationalists and their French colonial rulers. Backed by the Soviet Union, the nationalists defeated France and declared North Vietnam an independent communist state. The United States feared that communism might spread to other states. That would alter the balance of the Cold War, the struggle for political power between the United States and the Soviet Union.

U.S. Marines take shelter behind a partly destroyed wall during fighting for the central Vietnamese city of Hue.

Nationalists: People who believe in the right of a nation to govern itself.

Phosphorus bombs explode among enemy positions in May 1966. One U.S. commander said that he wanted to bomb Vietnam "back to the Stone Age."

UNEVEN TECHNOLOGY

From 1961 U.S. military advisors arrived to help the Army of South Vietnam (ARVN). Ground troops arrived in March 1965. The Americans and their allies faced the Army of North Vietnam (NVA) and a guerrilla force based in the South, called the Vietcong or VC.

On paper, U.S. military equipment was far superior to that of the enemy. But the terrain was hostile, and the enemy were skilled in jungle fighting and guerrilla warfare. North Vietnam avoided defeat until public opinion at home forced a U.S. withdrawal. In 1975, the war finally ended when North Vietnamese troops defeated the ARVN and captured Saigon, capital of South Vietnam.

Guerrilla: An irregular soldier who fights through ambush, sabotage, and assassination.

A-1 SKYRAIDER

Skyraiders fly in formation on a mission above the flat landscape of the Mekong Delta in southern Vietnam.

The Douglas A-1 Skyraider was a veteran attack aircraft. It first flew in 1945, at the very end of World War II. It was only meant to be in Vietnam as a stopgap. Instead, it lasted the whole war. It was the workhorse of the U.S. military and their allies in the South Vietnamese Airforce (SVAF). The Skyraider was tough and adaptable. It attacked at low altitude—just above treetops— often in the face of relentless antiaircraft fire. Pilots called the A-1 the "Spad" or "Able Dog."

Stopgap: A temporary fix for a problem.

TECHNICIANS load munitions beneath the wing of a Skyraider before a mission.

"ABLE DOG"

The propeller-driven A-1 was only capable of a top speed of 318 miles per hour (512 km/h). But it made up for being slow by being powerful. It could carry up to 8,000 pounds (3,270 kg) of bombs, cluster bombs, or chemicals such as napalm and phosphorus. It could also fire rockets and had two 20mm cannons.

Another benefit of the Skyraider was its ability to stay airborne longer and fly longer distances than other aircraft in the war. That made it perfect for carrying out search-and-rescue missions to locate soldiers behind enemy lines.

A Skyraider releases a napalm bomb as it approaches a target thought to be used by the Vietcong.

Cluster bombs: Bombs that contain a number of "bomblets" that all detonate together.

This Navy A-4 has been fitted with additional fuel tanks beneath the wings to increase its range.

A-4 SKYHAWK

The Douglas A-4 Skyhawk made some of the first air strikes in Vietnam; and a Marine Skyhawk dropped the last bombs of the war. Both the Marines and the Navy used the compact ground-attack aircraft. It could take off from aircraft carriers where there were no airbases. The "Bantam Bomber"—named for a lightweight boxer—flew more missions than any other U.S. naval aircraft.

Ground-attack aircraft: A warplane used to attack targets on the ground.

HOT ROD

The light bomber was sometimes called "Heinemann's Hot Rod" for its designer, Ed Heinemann. He wanted the aircraft to be light and simple to use. He made it half the weight of other bombers. That meant it was easy to maneuver but also fast. It set an air-speed record in 1954 of 695 miles per hour (1,120 km/h).

The planes had delta wings. They fit in the holds of aircraft carriers without having to be folded. Although it was so light, the A-4 had a punch: It could carry up to 8,200 pounds (3,720 kg) of bombs.

A pilot prepares for a mission on board an aircraft carrier. The planes' wings made them easy to store on carriers.

A technician loads 20mm ammunition for a Skyhawk's cannons.

EYEWITNESS

"I was off! Whoosh! It was like being shot from a sling. The initial surge pinned my head and body back against the seat. My eyeballs rattled and my vision blurred. It was more exhilarating than the plunge of a roller coaster."

Everett Alvarez, Jr.
1st U.S. pilot shot down in Vietnam

Delta wing: A wing shaped like a swept-back triangle.

A "Spooky" flies above Vietnam. The gunship's huge firing capacity could be used to fire flares to light up ground fighting at night.

AC-47 GUNSHIP

The AC-47 Gunship, as its name suggests, was a flying arsenal. The "Spooky" (also known as "Puff the Magic Dragon") was introduced in 1965. It was the first in a series of heavily armed gunships used by the U.S. Air Force in Vietnam. Its firepower allowed it to give ground troops close air support. It would fly wherever it was needed and could stay in the air for hours, if necessary.

Arsenal: A place for storing weapons.

"SPOOKY"

"Spooky" carried either three powerful miniguns or 10 machine guns, placed in the windows and a side door. The pilot could fire the guns all together or individually. The aircraft carried 24,000 rounds of ammunition.

It was said that a 3-second burst of gunfire could put one round in every square foot of a target as big as a football field. Such firepower terrified the enemy.

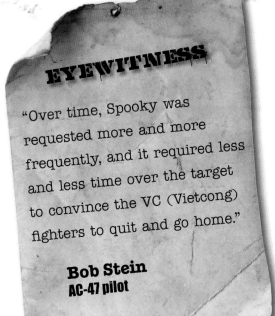

EYEWITNESS

"Over time, Spooky was requested more and more frequently, and it required less and less time over the target to convince the VC (Vietcong) fighters to quit and go home."

Bob Stein
AC-47 pilot

Tracer fire lights up the sky as AC-47s attack targets in a Vietnamese city.

The guns were mounted in the rear windows of the gunship; they could all be controlled by the pilot.

Minigun: A multi-barreled machine gun that can fire 2,000 to 6,000 rounds a minute.

AH-1 COBRA

Vietnam was the first helicopter war. Dense jungle and steep hills made it difficult for fixed-wing aircraft to land, but helicopters coped easily with the terrain. The Bell AH-1 Cobra—also known as the "HueyCobra" or the "Snake"—was the foundation of the U.S. Army's attack helicopter fleet. With a crew of two, the Cobra was the first helicopter gunship developed specifically for its job: supporting troops in the frontline.

The Cobra carried rockets and bombs beneath its stub wings and had a cannon mounted in a turret beneath the nose.

Gunship: A heavily armed helicopter or airplane.

COBRAS fly in formation low over the Vietnamese forest. Although heavily armed, they were vulnerable to antiaircraft fire.

A technician loads 70mm Folding Fin Aerial Rockets (FFARs) onto a Cobra.

ESCORT CHOPPER

The Cobra was first used in response to the North Vietnamese Tet Offensive in 1968. From then until the end of the war, Cobras clocked over a million hours of flying time. About 300 of the 1,100 choppers were lost. Over the course of the war, their design changed to minimize the chance of losses due to antiaircraft fire.

The job of the Cobra was to provide fire support for ground forces and to escort transport helicopters. As soldiers dropped to the ground, they were at risk of attack. The Cobra hovered close by. Its two multi-barreled guns, seven rockets, and 20mm cannon provided cover.

EYEWITNESS

"We flew much more reconnaissance than close air support, as we were the eyes of the division. We were always way out in front of our ground troops, looking for targets for them to exploit."

Chief Warrant Officer Randy Zhan
Commander, Cindy Ann Cobra

AK-47

The origins of the AK-47 assault rifle are given away by its alternative name: the Kalashnikov. Named after its inventor, the AK-47 Kalashnikov was produced in the Soviet Union. The Soviets supplied the rifles to their communist allies, the Army of North Vietnam (NVA) and the Vietcong (VC). But some U.S. soldiers preferred the AK-47 to their own M16 rifles. If they captured an AK-47, they often kept it and used it.

These AK-47s are part of a weapons hoard that was seized by U.S. troops during operations in South Vietnam.

Assault rifle: An automatic or semiautomatic gun that can hold many rounds of ammunition.

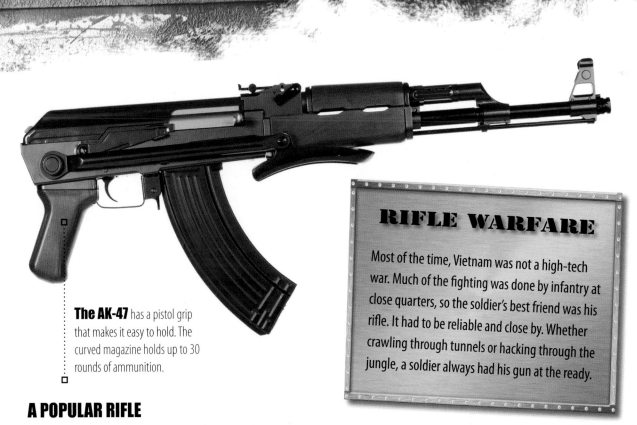

The AK-47 has a pistol grip that makes it easy to hold. The curved magazine holds up to 30 rounds of ammunition.

A POPULAR RIFLE

The AK-47 was cheap to produce and very reliable. It was easy to maintain. It worked well even in the steamy jungles of Vietnam, where other guns often jammed. The gun was also small and light and comfortable to carry on long marches.

The AK-47 was an automatic: This meant it fired continuously when the trigger was squeezed. A firing rate of 600 rounds per minute enabled any target to be raked with fire. The AK-47 is still in use today. Its popularity is clear from the total number that have been produced: 100 million.

This member of the Vietcong holds his AK-47 as he stands on top of a destroyed U.S. personnel carrier.

Rake: To sweep an area back and forth with gunfire.

MACHINES AND WEAPONRY OF THE VIETNAM WAR

Bombs rain from a B-52 above Vietnam. The airplane could carry up to 42 bombs in its hold and another 24 beneath its wings.

B-52 STRATOFORTRESS

The B-52 is probably the most successful military aircraft ever. It was designed in the early 1950s for high-altitude, long-range missions carrying nuclear bombs. The B-52 was a key part of the U.S. nuclear deterrent during the Cold War. For Vietnam, the heavy bomber was redesigned for lower-altitude bombing missions and to intercept surface-to-air missiles (SAMs).

Deterrent: A threat that deters, or prevents, the enemy from attacking.

B-52s drop their bombs on enemy positions from high altitude.

Incendiary bombs are loaded onto a B-52 ready to support a ground mission in February 1967.

MASSIVE AIRCRAFT

Everything about the B-52 was big. Its wingspan was 185 feet (56 m). It could carry 110,000 pounds (570 kg) of bombs. Its range was 3,000 miles (4,800 km). It bombed targets from a height of 22,000 feet (6.75 km). That was so high that often the first thing the enemy knew about a bomb was when it landed.

The B-52s disrupted enemy troop positions. They also supported ground troops. From June 1965 to August 1973, B-52s flew 124,532 sorties from bases in Guam and Thailand.

THUNDER

B-52s took part in Operation Rolling Thunder, the name given to a sustained bombing campaign against North Vietnam. The campaign began on March 2, 1965, and lasted until November 2, 1968. A massive 864,000 tons (785,000 t) of bombs were dropped on a range of targets. The campaign ended in failure because it did not force the North Vietnamese to give in.

Incendiary: Something designed to start a fire or cause a fire to spread.

C-47 CHINOOK

At the peak of the war, there were 22 Chinook units in Vietnam, flying about 750 two-rotor C-47 Chinooks. The Chinook's lifting ability was key to U.S. Army strategy. It got troops to remote locations where there were no roads. It could either land or hover while soldiers slid to the ground on ropes. The Chinook carried artillery weapons to positions high on mountains and took supplies to forward bases, often under heavy fire. It also evacuated casualties from the frontline to the hospital.

A Chinook comes in to land and evacuate troops from the frontline at a location marked by a smoke grenade.

Rotor: A blade that revolves at very high speed.

HEAVY LIFTER

A Chinook flight could keep a unit supplied for weeks with food and ammunition. The hold could carry up to 7,000 pounds (3,175 kg). Still, soldiers sometimes overloaded the helicopter in their eagerness to get supplies to forward positions. Then the aircraft could not take off.

The Chinook had one big disadvantage: It was so big that it was an easy target for enemy fire. The chopper had M60 machine guns on each side for protection. Flying a Chinook was still a dangerous job, however. Over a quarter of the helicopters were lost in the war.

EYEWITNESS

"I noticed there was no glass in the window openings. The crew chief said 'We have no machine guns on this aircraft. If we catch ground fire, stick your rifles out the window openings and fire back.'"

Raymond Cochran
Naval Seabee, attached to 3rd Marine Division

A CH-47 Chinook uses its cargo hook to bring in ammunition for a battery of 105mm howitzers during a search-and-destroy mission.

Cargo hook: A hook beneath an aircraft used to carry loads in a sling.

CHEMICAL WEAPONS

One of the most controversial aspects of the Vietnam War was the use of chemical weapons. U.S. commanders feared that enemy bases were hidden by thick forest. Aircraft sprayed chemicals to kill the vegetation, like weedkiller. Other chemical weapons targeted individuals, causing terrible injuries.

Bombs are filled with napalm at a U.S. airbase.

A Skyraider drops a phosphorus bomb on a target in February 1966. Phosphorus could burn skin very badly.

Chemical weapons: Weapons that cause burning, poisoning, irritation, or asphyxiation.

A huge explosion marks a napalm strike against suspected Vietcong positions.

CHEMICALS IN ACTION

From 1960 to 1973, airplanes sprayed 21 million gallons of Agent Orange. This toxic chemical stripped leaves from the rain forest. It was also sprayed on crops to try and starve the enemy.

Other U.S. bombs contained chemicals that caught fire, such as phosphorus. Napalm was an explosive petroleum jelly that stuck to the flesh. It caused horrible, deep burns. It was difficult to target accurately. Many Vietnamese civilians, including children, became victims of phosphorus and napalm.

Biological weapons: Weapons that use germs or herbicides in warfare.

As a daytime clear-weather fighter, The Super Sabre didn't need radar: The pilot located targets visually.

F-100 SUPER SABRE

The Super Sabre was the first U.S. Air Force jet fighter that could fly at supersonic speeds. Its main job was to escort other aircraft on bombing raids over North Vietnam. In South Vietnam, the Super Sabre used its speed to carry out close-air support and to make ground attacks. It dropped conventional and chemical bombs.

Supersonic: Faster than the speed of sound, or 768 miles per hour (1,236 km/h).

STURDY AIRPLANE

The F-100—nicknamed the "Hun"—was the longest serving jet fighter in Vietnam. It was in service from April 1961 until 1971. The aircraft were super reliable and tough, and easy to maintain and get in the air.

The aircraft could fly multiple missions every day, including spotting targets and search and rescue. The F-100's original job was air-to-air combat. It shot down its first North Vietnamese Air Force MiG-17 on April 4, 1965.

AN F-100 releases a napalm bomb over Vietcong positions.

MiG: A type of fighter plane built by the Soviet Union.

FLAMETHROWER

The flamethrower first appeared during World War II (1939–1945). At its most basic, it was a tank filled with gasoline that was strapped to a soldier's back. A nozzle led from the tank to a tube in the soldier's hands. When the trigger was pressed, a flame shot up to 65 feet (20 m) forward for about seven seconds. In the jungles of Vietnam, flamethrowers were used to terrify the enemy and to destroy vegetation.

A flame tank
fires a burst of napalm at a suspected enemy position near Saigon in early 1968.

Napalm: A kind of explosive jelly that sticks to the skin and causes terrible burns.

A stream of fire shoots from a U.S. boat on a river in Vietnam. Flamethrowers cleared vegetation along the riverbanks.

MOUNTED FLAMETHROWERS

By the time of the Vietnam War, larger flamethrowers were mounted on tanks or on the boats of the "Brown Water Navy." They were used to burn off the vegetation along Vietnam's rivers.

These mounted flamethrowers had a much longer range than handheld weapons. The fuel tanks were larger, too, so flame attacks could last longer. The flamethrowers used gasoline to burn buildings or clear away vegetation. They also shot napalm as an antipersonnel weapon.

ZIPPOS

The deadly U.S. flameboats that sailed along Vietnamese rivers were nicknamed "Zippos," for a popular brand of cigarette lighter. Guns mounted in revolving turrets shot streams of flaming napalm up to 200 yards (180 m) onto the banks. The "Zippos" supported land operations. The flames destroyed anything within range—but that sometimes included villages and homes.

Range: The distance a weapon can fire and still be effective.

M16 RIFLE

From early 1967, the M16 was the standard rifle for U.S. infantrymen in Vietnam. It was intended to rival the enemy's highly successful AK-47. At 6½ pounds (2.95 kg), it was lighter than the M14, which it replaced. That made it easier to carry. It was also easy to use and to reload. On automatic, it could fire between 750 and 900 rounds per minute, up to a range of 470 yards (430 m).

A soldier takes aim with his M16, which has been adapted with the addition of a grenade launcher beneath the barrel.

Grenade launcher: A wide-barreled small-arms weapon that fires small bombs.

An ARVN soldier fires his M16 during a firefight. The Americans equipped their Vietnamese allies with the rifles.

A Special Forces soldier on boat patrol on a Vietnamese river has a cover around the barrel of his M16 to keep it dry.

JUNGLE READY?

Not all soldiers were happy with their new rifles. The first M16s were not suited to the tropical Vietnamese climate. The gun worked best when it was clean and dry. But it was hard to keep it that way in the jungle. The rifle got wet and dirty—and then it jammed. It was still jamming at the siege of Khe Sahn in 1968.

As the war went on, the teething problems were ironed out. The gun became more reliable. Modifications like the M16A1 worked better. They could be fitted with a grenade launcher beneath the barrel. The M16 became the standard U.S. infantry rifle until it was phased out in 2010.

EYEWITNESS

"I decided that the M16 was essential, not only for the American troops but for the Vietnamese. I made such a request in December 1965."

Gen. William Westmoreland
Commander, U.S. Military Operations, Vietnam

Firefight: A brief, intense exchange of fire between two military units.

27

M-48s of the U.S. 5th Cavalry Regiment search for North Vietnamese soldiers after the Tet Offensive in 1968.

M-48 PATTON TANK

Named for the World War II general, George S. Patton, the M-48 medium tank was the largest U.S. tank in Vietnam. Although more than 600 were sent to Vietnam, few tank-to-tank battles took place. The Patton was used to support infantry actions in the jungle and also in Vietnamese towns and cities. It had a top speed of up to 30 miles per hour (48 km/h) and was armed with a main gun and two machine guns.

Tet Offensive: A surprise North Vietnamese attack on cities throughout the South in January 1968.

NO TANK WAR

Vietnam was not a war for tanks. The landscape didn't suit tank combat: It was too hilly and the vegetation was too thick. The Army of North Vietnam and the Vietcong had few tanks until late in the war.

The Patton made itself useful anyway. It guarded convoys, supported troops in combat, and secured strategic routes. At night, tanks and armored personnel carriers (APCs) were used to encircle a camp to protect soldiers from the enemy. The tank was adaptable: It could be fitted with flamethrowers for clearing vegetation.

EYEWITNESS

"North Vietnamese small arms fire was hitting the tank and flying all around me. Later, after the battle was over, I saw that my helmet had several places where some rounds had gotten close to my skull."

Dwight W. Birdwell
Tank commander, winner of the Silver Heart

M-48 Patton tanks of the 11th Armored Cavalry Regiment are moved by barge along one of Vietnam's rivers.

M-48 tanks and armored personnel carriers (APCs) advance in search of the enemy during an operation to destroy Vietcong headquarters.

M60 MACHINE GUN

The M60 was a general-purpose machine gun that saw widespread action in Vietnam. The gun was light enough to carry on patrol—but only just. It usually took a crew of two or three to carry the gun and its ammunition. U.S. infantrymen called it "the Pig," because it was heavy and "ate" ammunition at a huge rate. The gun could also be fixed onto helicopters or tanks, as needed. First used in 1957, it is still in use today.

Dug-in with an ample supply of cartridge belts, a U.S. soldier prepares to face the enemy.

Patrol: A military mission carried out for reconnaissance or to maintain security.

UH-1 Hueys armed with M60 machine guns fly a search-and-destroy mission over Quan Rhu Tuc.

A machine-gun team from the 3rd Battalion, 5th Marine Regiment, fires on the enemy in the 1968 Tet Offensive.

JAMMED GUNS

A major problem for many of the soldiers in Vietnam was a weapon that jammed in the middle of combat. In a firefight, this could be fatal. Soldiers complained that they could not rely on guns such as the M60 or the M16 rifle in times of danger. The U.S. Army responded by continually improving models to iron out the technical difficulties, but this wasn't always successful. Soldiers had to work extra hard to keep their guns clean.

HEAVYWEIGHT WEAPON

The M60 could be fired from the shoulder or the hip in short bursts, but the firer soon got tired. For greater accuracy, it could be supported on a bipod that was built into the barrel or on a separate tripod. It fired up to 550 high-velocity bullets to a range of 1,900 yards (1,740 m).

There were two major complaints about the M60. First, the weight of the cartridge belt limited how much ammunition could be carried. Every man in a company helped by carrying up to 200 rounds. Second, like other U.S.-made guns, the M60 tended to jam in damp, dirty battlefield conditions.

Search-and-destroy: A mission to find enemy positions and attack them.

M-60 TANK

The M-60 Patton tank was intended to be an improvement on the M-48. It was introduced in December 1960 and remained one of the world's most successful main battle tanks until 1997. It didn't play much of a role in Vietnam. Most of the time, the ground was too muddy for it to operate effectively. Its main task was to destroy fortified North Vietnamese Army and Vietcong positions close to settlements.

The main gun of the M-60 Patton was the 105mm M68. A Combat Brigade version used in Vietnam had a bulldozer attachment at the front.

Main battle tank: The heaviest and most powerfully armed class of tanks.

Commanders in a column of M-60s raise their arms to warn the tanks behind them to come to a halt.

HEAVY DUTY

The M-60 was far bigger than any tank operated by the NVA, but it didn't fight many tank-on-tank battles. It could deliver firepower in situations that weren't suitable for airpower. It was also useful for securing roads and cutting off enemy routes.

The M-60's turret held a 105mm M68 main gun and a machine gun. Its sides were covered in steel armor up to 6 inches (15 cm) thick. It was the last tank to have an escape hatch under the hull.

SPECIAL TANKS

One of the most useful variants of the M-60 tank used in Vietnam was the AVLB (armored vehicle launch bridge) tank. It was an M-60 that carried a folded scissors bridge. The bridge could be extended to a total span of 60 feet (18 m). It was very useful, particularly in the Mekong Delta, where there were many waterways blocking the U.S. advance.

Armor: A protective covering of metal or ceramics that protects something from blows.

M79 GRENADE LAUNCHER

Infantrymen in Vietnam found it tough to dislodge a dug-in, often invisible enemy with rifles and machine guns alone. They needed to increase their firepower. The answer was the M79, a shoulder-fired grenade launcher. The M79 made a distinctive sound when it fired. That earned it nicknames like "blooper," "thumper," "thump gun," and "bloop tube". The Australians called it the "wombat gun."

Soldiers of the 4th Infantry Division use M79s during an operation in Quang Ngai province in 1967.

Dug-in: Occupying well-guarded and fortified positions such as trenches.

VERSATILE WEAPON

The M79 was designed for carrying. It weighed just 6 pounds (2.72 kg). But being small didn't mean that it lacked power. It could fire grenades up to 385 yards (350 m) and was powerful enough to stop light armored vehicles. It was ideal for jungle terrain. Grenades helped to flush the enemy out from their defensive positions. They could be fired from such a long range that they took the enemy by surprise.

The M79 had one significant drawback that soldiers found maddening. It could only fire a single grenade before it had to be reloaded. That meant the weapon was useless in close-combat situations.

EYEWITNESS

"The M79 was very popular because it was fun and easy to shoot. It was a deadly little dude. It looked like a small, breechloading, sawed-off shotgun."

Clair William Clark II
Missileer

An Australian special forces soldier teaches a South Vietnamese recruit to fire an M79.

Missileer: A soldier whose job it is to operate missiles and rockets.

35

M107 HOWITZER

One nickname sums up the importance of the M107 howitzer in Vietnam: the "king of the battle." The howitzer was used from early in the war to provide long-range fire support. The M107 was highly effective. It had the longest range of any mobile artillery weapon of the period. In the right conditions, it could fire a 147-pound projectile up to 21 miles (34 km).

The M107 had a crew of 13; when it was traveling, only the driver was protected by the vehicle's armor.

Howitzer: An artillery gun that fires shells in a high arc, to pass over enemy defenses.

Hidden by a camouflage net, an M107 of the 3rd Marine Division shells Vietcong positions in 1965.

The huge shells of the M109 were able to penetrate the thick canopy of the Vietnamese jungle.

A KEY PLAYER

Each M107 had a crew of 13 men. If it was driven around, it had an operational range of 450 miles (725 km). Often, however, the self-propelled howitzers were dug in to their positions. The M107 was used at artillery firebases throughout South Vietnam.

At the siege of Khe Sanh, a U.S. Marine firebase was surrounded by North Vietnamese forces for months. The M107 played a vital role in defending the firebase from the ongoing enemy attacks.

FIREBASES

Firebases, or fire support bases, were forward artillery placements. They provided artillery support for troops far from their own bases. Originally the firebases were temporary, but many became semi-permanent. They were often in remote locations, surrounded by the enemy. Each base usually had six howitzers, as well as engineers to maintain the guns and a helicopter-landing pad so that supplies could be flown in.

Self-propelled: A gun that has an engine and wheels or tracks, so it can move on its own.

M113 ARMORED PERSONNEL CARRIER

The M113 Armored Personnel Carrier (APC) was the backbone of armored cavalry formations. By January 1968, there were 2,100 in Vietnam. Their tanklike tracks coped easily with muddy terrain. They could "swim" across rivers or lakes. They could be transported by air and parachuted into combat zones.

ARVN crew maneuver an M113 APC during an advance; it is armed with a Browning M2 machine gun.

Armored cavalry: Units that used mechanized vehicles to make rapid advances.

Soldiers head for the safety of their APCs during a patrol in hostile territory.

Infantry advance cautiously under cover of M113s.

BATTLEFIELD TAXI

The M113's job was to get infantry into battle. It could carry 11 fully equipped soldiers, as well as a driver and machine gunner or commander. The vehicle could also be easily modified for any number of uses. It could carry mortars, machine guns, flamethrowers, command posts, or whatever was needed. It was a jack-of-all-trades.

The M113 had a top land speed of 40 miles per hour (64 km/h) and 4 miles per hour (6.4 km/h) in water. It was vital for search-and-rescue missions. It was also used in most large-scale advances in the war. It was useful because it could pursue the enemy across any terrain.

EYEWITNESS

"My M113 had all sorts of quirks, like spraying diesel fuel into the driver's compartment and using a couple of gallons of water a day. Maintenance gave up trying to find the leak. I got used to the little things and planned around them."

William Kestell
4/23rd Infantry (Mechanized),
25th Infantry Division

Mortar: A cannon that fires projectiles at a high angle.

M551 SHERIDAN

The Sheridan was light compared to main battle tanks, so it could be easily airlifted into combat zones.

Most of the time, tanks were not suited to fighting in Vietnam. One exception was the Sheridan. This light amphibious battle tank first arrived in Vietnam in January 1969. It had the great advantage of weighing only 25 tons (22.6 t). That meant it could be parachuted into any combat zone where the terrain allowed tanks to be effective.

Amphibious: Able to operate equally well on land or in water.

AN ADAPTABLE TANK

The Sheridan was not intended for jungle combat. It operated best in towns and cities. But it proved very adaptable. Its main gun was the 152mm M81. It fired M625 canister shells that could cut through the thick Vietnamese jungle and blow apart bamboo thickets.

Some Sheridan crews rode on top of the tank. They risked being shot at—but they preferred it to being inside. The tanks' aluminum armor was thin. If they hit enemy landmines, the tanks could easily blow up. The soldiers reckoned it was easier to jump off a Sheridan to fight than to be trapped inside a burning furnace.

EYEWITNESS

"If you got hit by a rocket-propelled grenade in a Sheridan turret and it got into the caseless ammunition, it was just a powder keg. The Sheridan guys kind of feared that a bit."

Charles T. Dodge
1 Troop, 11th Armored Cavalry Regiment (Texas Tech Archive)

An M551 Sheridan of the 11th Armored Cavalry Regiment patrols near Hung Loc in early 1971.

Landmine: A buried bomb that is detonated by weight being applied on top.

MONITOR

Vietnam has 3,000 miles (4,800 km) of inland waterways: rivers, canals, estuaries, and lakes. They were often lined by thick jungle that hid enemy movements. The Monitor patrolled these dangerous waters. The command and communications vessel was named for the USS *Monitor*, a Civil War gunship with a revolving turret. Like its namesake, the Monitor was heavily armored.

A heavily armed Monitor leads an assault flotilla along a river in the Mekong Delta.

Flotilla: A limited naval unit comprising small warships.

Twin 12.7mm machine guns mounted on a U.S. Navy river patrol boat on the Vung Tau River.

Monitors (with forward turrets) and Armored Troop Carriers are moored alongside a larger ship in the Mekong Delta.

MOBILE RIVERINE FORCE

The Monitor was a converted landing craft from World War II. In case of attack, it was heavily armed with machine guns, grenade launchers, mortars, and even howitzers. The vessel was heavy and strong, but its shallow draft meant it could sail in shallow waters.

The Monitor led the Mobile Riverine Force (MRF), which was formed in 1969. Its job was to stop the enemy using waterways to resupply Vietcong guerrillas in the delta. The boats opened up parts of the delta that were inaccessible any other way.

RIVER FORCE

The Brown Water Navy got its name from Vietnam's muddy rivers. The rivers acted as highways for enemy transportation. The Mobile Riverine Force (MRF) tried to intervene. The MRF combined U.S. Army troops with crews from the U.S. Navy. Its vessels included not only Monitors, but also fast patrol boats, armored gunboats, troop carriers, and napalm-firing boats.

Draft: The depth of a boat's hull below the waterline.

A gunner keeps lookout as a Navy Huey flies a patrol. The helicopter carried various weapons, including the M60 machine gun.

UH-1 HUEY

Vietnam is often called the "helicopter war"—and the main helicopter of the conflict was the Huey. It supported the whole U.S. war effort. The Huey was everywhere because it was perfect for the jungle. It could fly low above the ground and at low speeds. It could land in small clearings, could be maneuvered to dodge enemy fire, and was heavily armed. It had a crew of two and could carry seven soldiers.

EYEWITNESS

"At 50 feet from touchdown we were met by heavy automatic weapons fire but continued on in ... the explosion tore at the left front of the cockpit."

Wiliam Dismukes
Pilot, 173rd Assault Helicopter Company

Cockpit: The part of an aircraft where the pilot sits.

HEAVY USE

The Bell UH-1 Huey—its designation was originally HU-1—transported troops, equipment, supplies, and support personnel. It provided additional firepower for ground actions and was used as an air ambulance to evacuate injured troops. It also carried out search-and-rescue, reconnaissance, and propaganda missions.

The first Hueys arrived in Vietnam in 1962 with U.S. Army medics. Eventually, about 7,000 Hueys served in Vietnam. The chopper was continually upgraded and adapted to meet different needs. All arms of the U.S. military flew Hueys: the Army, Air Force, Navy, and the Marine Corps.

Hueys of the 101st Airborne Division lay a smoke screen . A top speed of 127 miles per hour (204 km/h) meant the Huey could quickly deploy to support ground operations.

A Huey hovers above the ground as casualties are loaded on makeshift stretchers for evacuation from the front line.

Propaganda: Material that tries to encourage support or to demoralize the enemy.

GLOSSARY

amphibious: Able to operate equally well on land or in water.

arsenal: A place for storing weapons.

chemical weapons: Weapons that cause burning, poisoning, irritation, or asphyxiation.

cluster bombs: Bombs that contain a number of "bomblets" that all detonate together.

delta wing: A wing shaped like a swept-back triangle.

deterrent: A threat that deters, or prevents, the enemy from attacking.

draft: The depth of a boat's hull beneath the waterline.

dug-in: Occupying well-guarded and fortified positions such as trenches.

fire support: Providing additional or covering fire for forces on the ground.

firefight: A brief, intense exchange of fire.

ground-attack aircraft: A warplane used to attack targets on the ground.

guerrilla: An irregular soldier who fights through ambush, sabotage, and assassination.

gunship: A heavily armed helicopter or airplane.

howitzer: An artillery gun that fires shells in a high arc, to pass over enemy defenses.

incendiary: Something designed to start a fire or cause a fire to spread.

landmine: A buried bomb that is detonated when weight is applied on top.

main battle tank: The heaviest and most powerfully armed class of tanks.

MiG: A type of fighter plane built by the Soviet Union.

minigun: A multi-barreled machine gun.

mortar: A cannon that fires projectiles at a high angle.

napalm: A kind of explosive jelly that sticks to the skin and causes terrible burns.

patrol: A military mission carried out for reconnaissance or to maintain security.

rake: To sweep an area back and forth with gunfire.

range: The distance a weapon can fire and still be effective.

rotor: A blade that revolves at very high speed.

stopgap: A temporary fix for a problem.

strategic: Concerned with the overall aims of a war, not just the immediate battle.

supersonic: Faster than the speed of sound, or 768 miles per hour (1,235 km/h).

FURTHER INFORMATION

BOOKS

Baker, David. *M113 Armored Personnel Vehicle* (Fighting Forces on Land). Rourke Publishing, 2006.

Green, Michael, and Gladys Green. *Heavy Bombers: The B-52 Stratofortress* (Edge Books: War Planes). Capstone Press, 2008.

Hemingway, Al. *American Naval Forces in the Vietnam War* (The American Experience in Vietnam). World Almanac Library, 2005.

Kent, Deborah. *The Vietnam War: From Da Nang to Saigon* (United States at War). Enslow Publishers, 2011.

Tougas, Shelley. *Weapons, Gear, and Uniforms of the Vietnam War.* Capstone Press, 2012.

Wiest, Andrew. *The Vietnam War* (Essential Histories). Rosen Publishing Group, 2008.

WEBSITES

http://www.history.com/topics/ weapons-of-the-vietnam-war
History.com descriptions of major weapons, plus links to videos.

http://military.discovery.com/ history/vietnam-war/vietnam-war.html
Military Channel guide to weapons, vehicles, and individuals.

http://www.pbs.org/wgbh/amex/ vietnam/trenches/weapons.html
PBS site to support the TV show *The American Experience.*

http://www.pbs.org/battlefieldvietnam
PBS site to support the TV series *Battlefield Vietnam.*

http://www.historyplace.com/ unitedstates/vietnam
The History Place Vietnam War site with timelines and links.

INDEX